Guide

Paloma Esteban Leal
Chief curator of the Collections

Museo Nacional Centro de Arte Reina Sofía

ALDEASA

the collection

*T*heir Royal Majesties Don Juan Carlos and Doña Sofía, inaugurated on the 10th of September 1992, the Permanent Collection of the Museo Nacional Centro de Arte Reina Sofía, which, up to now, had housed only temporary exhibitions. From such date onwards, it would constitute an actual Museum, with tasks of maintenance, increase and exhibition of its own artistic funds.

However, the origin of the building housing the MNCARS, dates back far away on time. After several prior vicissitudes, on the second half of the XVIIIth century, the project for a Hospital was commissioned to the architect Francisco Sabatini, who, nevertheless, could not fully finish the building, raising only part of that planned on the plans. From then on, and virtually until the present time, the Hospital was modified and even enlarged with some additions, and did survive, in spite of several opinions that claimed for its demolition, since it was appointed historical-artistic monument by a Royal Decres of 1977.

The restoration of the building starts in 1980, carried out by Antonio Fernández Alba, and, at the end of 1988, José Luis Iñiguez de Onzoño and Antonio Vázquez de Castro undertook the last modifications, mainly outstanding among them, the three glass and steel elevator towers, designed in collaboration with the British architect Ian Ritchie.

Two years earlier, in 1986, part of the still denominated «Centro de Arte Reina Sofía» facilities were inagurated, being this Centro only dedicated by then, to organize temporary

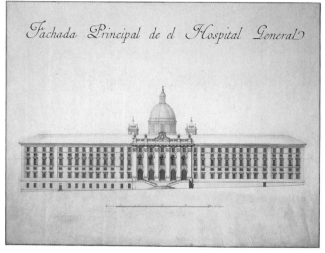

Elevation of the main façade. Francisco Sabatini.

activities, under the management of Carmen Giménez in her role of responsabilty of the «Centro Nacional de Exposiciones» of Ministry of Cultura.

Briefly thereafter, in 1988, a Royal Decree transformed the Centre into a National Museum replacing the, till this moment, «Museo Español de Arte Contemporáneo» (MEAC). Its first Director, that would be running the Institution from June 1988 to December 1990, was Tomás Llorens, who prosecuted the exhibition activity, and also inagurated the Library and the Documentation Center, located on the third floor and with a data resource available to the public through computerized systems.

Tomás Llorens was replaced in his post by María de Corral, on December 28, 1990. The Museum, under the new management, became an autonomous agency at the beginning of 1991.

The MNCARS artistic funds originate from two sources — as

Restoration of the building. Courtyard.

stated in the mentioned Royal Decree of 1988 which
transformed the Centro de Arte Reina Sofía into a National
Museum – the original MEAC's collections and pieces acquired
by the MNCARS itself.
Likewise, already in 1988, there was a hint as to the
possibility of transferring the xxth century pieces then located
at the Prado Museum, specially those referring to the Picasso's
«Guernica». Finally, this project became a reality in July 1992.
It must be mentioned, also related to the MNCARS' funds,
the legacies received by the Centro, highlighting among them,
those constituted, respectively, by Salvador Dalí's and Joan
Miro's works. The first endowment was stated as such in the
Cadaqués artist's last will, in 1982, which includes fifty-six
of his works. That of Miró comes mainly from the first
implementation of the Spanish Act of Historical Patrimony
concerning inheritance rights (payment of the state duty),
put into practice in 1985.

Some works of the Permanent Collection
may be substituted by other piedes, not
incluided in the guide, due to the temporal
loans that the MNCARS realizes to take
part of diverse exhibitions.

1

③

②

①

*T*he opening space of the Permanent Collection
intends to show a selection of those names and
trends that constituted the Spanish artistic scene of the
beginning of the xxth century, that is, of those figures forming
the immediate precedent of the Avant-Garde, described
by some critics as «ahead of Modernity».
At the end of the xixth century, there existed in Spain two
fundamental plastic cores, that developed, almost
simultaneously, in Catalonia and the Basque Country,
although showing great differences between them.
This room exhibits some samples of the most outstanding
components of both artistic focuses — the Basque and the
Catalonian — such as Nonell, Anglada Camarasa, Iturrino,
Echevarría or Zuloaga, together with pieces of other artists
like María Blanchard or Julio González, who without really
sharing the plastic premises characteristic of the mentioned
Basque or Catalonian artists, also collaborated, from other
stances, to the progress in our country of the contemporary art
history, not forgetting, of course, the masterly figure of
Pablo Picasso.

PICASSO

Pablo Ruiz Picasso

He was born in Málaga in 1881. He died in Mougins, France, in 1973. His work, doubtless the most important artistic output produced in our century, goes through numerous and interesting stages, from the first one, the so-called blue period *(1901-1904), up to one of his latest series, that of the* famous pictures interpretation *(1955-1961), not forgetting, of course, the* pink period *(1905-1906), the* cubist period *(1908-1916), the return to the representation of strong Greek-Latin evocations (1917-1924), or the period near to the Surrealism (1925-1935), just to quote some of the mentioned stages. His best known and most emblematic work is the famous canvas* Guernica *(1937), piercing and fierce claim against the barbarity of the war.*

Pablo Picasso
Mujer en azul, 1901
(Woman in blue)
Oil on canvas
133 × 100 cm
Cat.no. 01618

This beautiful canvas was realized in one of the two brief stays of the Malagan artist in Madrid, between the end of the XIXth century and the beginning of the XXth century; it has a peculiar story. It was presented by its author to the National Exhibit of Fine Arts, in 1901, and after obtaining as a sole reward an honourable mention, Picasso, once the competition was over, decided not to pick it up. As time went by, several decades later, it was located and saved from oblivion by Enrique Lafuente Ferrari, becoming a part of the Spanish State's contemporaneous art collections. It shows a woman in pompous dress that seems to observe the onlooker through her enigmatic eyes.

ANGLADA
CAMARASA
·······································
Hermenegildo Anglada
Camarasa

*Born in Barcelona in 1871
he died in Pollensa, in
1959. During the last years
of the XIXth century, he
settled in the French capital
city, discovering the Paris
night life, which will
become one of his predilect
topics in his first period.
After his sucessfull
exhibitions in Belgium,
Germany, England, Italy
and France, he settled in
Pollensa, coinciding with
the beginning of the First
World War. His painting,
starting at first of a
naturalist style's
landscaping, will slowly
transform up to the
moment where the large
canvas appear, specially the
female portraits, of moderne
inspiration and bright
colouring.*

② ···

Hermenegildo Anglada Camarasa
Retrato de Sonia de Klamery,
Condesa de Pradére
(Portrait of Sonia de Klamery,
Countess of Pradére), a.1913
Oil on canvas
187 × 200 cm.
Cat.no. 00629

Anglada Camarasa's canvas identifie at the end of the
XIXth century, there existed in Spain two fundamental
plastic cores, with the modernist world, then in vogue in
his native Catalonia. From 1907 onwards, he depicts on
his works the cabaret's night life, full of translucent and
opalescent women, exalted by the painter to a category
of real living jewels.

The Russian Diaghilev's Ballet arrived in Paris, in 1909
with Nijinski and Paulova as prime dancers. This event,
constituted a social and artistic happening, that will
cause a revolution in tastes and habits. Anglada will be
deeply impressed by the sceneries and wardrobes, of
extremaly vivid orange, fuchsia, green colours..., to such
a point that, since then, the multicoloured glitter will
replace the pale shades in his female pictures, as
happens, for instance, in this *Portrait of Sonia Klamery.*

BLANCHARD

María Gutiérrez
Blanchard

She was born in Santander, in 1881. She died in Paris, in 1932. In 1908 she decided to move to the French capital city, where she will coincide with Hermenegildo Anglada Camarasa and with Juan Gris, with the latter she will share a dearly friendship. Her style on the years prior to the First World War, leans towards a kind of Expressionism with intense shades and dense material. The most decisive stage of her pictorial work starts from 1916 on, under the influence, mainly, of Juan Gris, developing a special Cubism manner. From 1920 onwards, she slowly yields the cubist rigour on her work arriving to a figurative canvas series, full of melancholy and sorrowful characters.

3

Maria Blanchard
La comulgante, 1914
(The Communicant)
Oil on canvas
180 × 124 cm
Cat.no. 07281

This oil was shown in the Independents Room of Paris, in 1921, having a remarkable sucess in the specialized critic. Its performance dates from years in which the painter's style moves towards an expressive use and distorted application of colour, as well as for the application of a coat of a dense and compact pictorial material, applied, sometimes, by means of the palette. Shortly before *The Communicant*'s performance, the Mexican painter Diego Rivera had travelled to Spain, working then in a series of totally figurative compositions —very different from his cubist paintings of 1914 —, made up with extremely bright colours, which might have been comtemplated later on in Paris by Maria Blanchard, serving her as inspiration in her work, in some ways so close to the Mexican popular art.

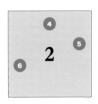

*N*ext to the topic devoted to the early years of our century, although occupying a totally independent area, lies the room including the work of José Gutiérrez Solana, an artist who, although isolated by own conviction from everything meaning Avant-Garde, he is one of the most original contemporary artists, since he goes beyond the academic limits, flowing into a sort of peculiar Expressionism.

Besides being an engraver, draughtsman and sporadic sculptor, Solana is mainly an excellent painter, who nourishes himself on subjects of his daily environment, although always transformed and recreated with his peculiar way of interpreting the world. Among said subjects, three groups could be specially outlined: those related to characters, streets and Madrilenian popular festivities — basically the carnivals —, those touching the usages and habits of the Black Spain, and the portraits.

The aggregate of works included in Solana's room of the Permanent Collection, is an exact reflection of the painter's plastic idiosyncrasy, perhaps standing out The Coterie at Café Pombo *(1920).*

SOLANA

José Gutiérrez Solana

He was born in Madrid in 1886 and also died, in 1945, in the same city. Very keen of the Madrilenian coteries, he attended to several of them, like in the Café de Levante or in the Café de Pombo, the latter immortalized in one of his most important canvases. Together with his painting work, his literary work also stands out, like the volume entitled Madrid. Scenes and Customs, *published in 1913. His personal style, very tied up to the Expressionism, is directly inspired through the contemplation of the Spanish painters' «Siglo de Oro». His aesthetic participates, to some extent, of the* Generación del 98 *pathetic vision about Spain of that period.*

José Gutierrez Solana
La tertulia del Café de Pombo, 1920
(The coterie at Café Pombo)
Oil on canvas
162 × 211,5 cm
Cat.no. 00915

This painting, Ramón Gómez de la Serna's donation in 1947 to the Spanish State, had been already exhibited in the Ist Salón de Otoño, before hanged in the later Museo de Arte Contemporáneo, happened in 1920 in the famous Madrilenian Café after which name this picture was named.

Among the people shown on it, there are dignataries in Arts and Literature's of the time, grouped around said Ramón Gómez de la Serna, who appears in the center of the painting. The dignataries mentioned are Manuel Abril, Tomás Borrás, José Bergamín, José Cabrero, Mauricio Bacarisse, Pedro Emilio Coll, Salvador Bartolozzy and Solana himslef, who auto-portraits in a magnificent show of pictorial performance.

13

⑤ ....

José Gutiérrez Solana
La visita del Obispo,
1926
(The Bishop's visit)
Oil on canvas
161 × 211 cm
Cat. no. 00566

This canvas, presented by Solana to the National Exhibition of Fine Arts of 1926, is also known as *The Bishop's family.* One of its most remarkable characteristics is the peculiar layout of the persons, all placed forming a semicircle around the figure who constitutes the axis of the scene — the Bishop —, and leaving sort of an open area — the second half of the circle — in the foreground of the picture, space through which the communication flows between the onlooker and the personages of the canvas.

The way of lighting the composition, by a beam of artificial light, arising from a kind of focus located on the upside of the canvas, contributes to the feeling of an atmosphere frozen on time that seems to emanate from both the people and its enviroment.

⑥ ....

José Gutiérrez Solana
La procesión de la
muerte, 1930
(The Death Procession)
Oil on canvas
209 × 123 cm
Cat. no. 00871

The magnetism that the phenomenon of death effected in Solana, is clearly shown in representations such as this canvas, which became part of the State Collections in 1945. The painter pays here homage to a certain Hispanic tradition as macabre as his own works and basically inspired in the Valdés Leal's *Vanitas.* The impressive baroque compositions, realized with the only purpose of reminding the spectator of life's brevity and death's certainty, revive again in scenes like this or in others alike, also carried out by Solana, fundamentally between 1920 and 1931.

*D*eemed by some of today's sculptors as «the father of this century's iron sculpture», Julio González is the creator of a work which importance lies mainly in two fundamental factors: the use of iron as artistic material — up to then, this material had just been considered appropiate to industrial purposes —, and the comparison of the void and the full, of space and form, as plastic elements that, brought together, shape the three dimensional work in equal shares. Goldsmith, painter, draughtsman and specially sculptor, Julio González starts using, towards 1929, the technique that would mean a revolutionary change for his creations: the forged, cut, curved and soldered iron.

The monograph room dedicated to his work in the Permanent Collection context, groups together as much paintings of a marked noucentist influence and strong vigour on strokes, as interesting drawings, either abstracts or figuratives, and specially, magnificent sculptures generally inspired in the cubist aesthetic.

7 ....

Julio González
La longue chevelure, 1939
(The Long Hair)
Indian ink by pen, wash and traces of pencil
on clear ochre paper
28 × 14,5 cm
Cat. no. 03041

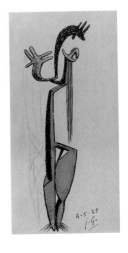

This drawing is one of the multifarious sketches realized
by the artist in the period 1939-40, related to the
Madame Cactus sculpture, made in the same period and
constituting the second version of the famous *Monsieur
Cactus*, of 1939.
In fact, *The Long Hair* is a cactus silhouette
metamorphosed into sinuous femenine curves in
accordance with the Surrealist tradition and, according
to some critics' opinion, Julio González could had been
inspired, as much for *Madame Cactus*' realization as for
its preparatory drawings, in an oil of the French painter
Jules Lefebvre titled *The Truth*, of 1870, in which precisely
a long-haired woman appears holding a mirror in her
raised arm.

8 ....

Julio González
Tête dite «Le Lapin», a. 1930
(Head called «The Rabbit»)
Soldered iron
33 × 17,5 × 111,5 cm
Cat. no. 10351

This work belongs to the series of pieces realized about
1930 by Julio González in cutted plate, all of them
mounted on calcareous stone uneven basements,
material also used somewhat later by his author, to carry
out his heads «ronde-bosse» (free-standing).
Possibly this bust, in which irony and humour are
present, could correspond to a self-portrait, considering
the represented personage's bushy eyebrows and his
very peculiar moustache, identifying marks of the
sculptor's physiognomy.

GONZÁLEZ

Julio González

He was born in Barcelona in 1876. He passed away in Arcueil, Paris in 1942. Through his job as welder's apprentice, he learned the welding technique, which will determine, from then onwards, his work as a sculptor. His creation, from 1928 on, showing till then cubist reminiscences, began to evolve towards abstract shapes known as «drawing in space». Between the end of the Twenties and beginning of the Thirties, he worked together with Pablo Picasso and in 1937 he realized his famous sculpture Montserrat *for the Spanish Pavilion of the World Fair of Paris of that year.*

9

Julio González
Les Amoureux II, 1932-1933
(The Lovers II)
Bronze
44 × 18,5 × 22 cm
Cat. no. 03108

This piece, realized about 1932-1933, is formed by two clearly delimited blocks — a kind of triangular silhouette base and a semi-ovoid bulk leaning in the mentioned base —, but forming a sole unit, unique and enveloping, in which the traditional dichotomy front/back, characteristic of the three-dimensional works, has been replaced by a global conception of the work.

Moreover, the collaboration between Picasso and Julio González takes place from 1928 to 1931, which will result in a profitable exchange of opinions by both sides. According to some specialists, the subject inspiring this sculpture, the kiss, understood as a sort of geometric symmetrical association, might come from Picasso's sculptures and oils realized on these same years.

4

*W*ith the appearance of the cubist movement,
the two great aesthetic courses that will, in good
part, conform the xxth century artistic avant-garde, the
subjective trend — Expressionism, Metaphysical Painting,
Dadaism or Surrealism — and the so-called objective trend
that, lead by the Cubism itself, the Orfism or the Futurism,
will originate later on the different rationalisms.
The cubist painters will find out that the way of depiction
known as renacentist perspective — assuming that the human
vision was monocular, fixed and instantaneous — was not the
only possible one, bringing as a contrast on their canvases, the
binocular vision system and the possible different points of
view of a same motif, grouped in a sole composition. Because
of the importance given to the way of depiction, the depicted
passes to a second level and the subject itself lacks importance.
The colour will not be important either, being basically
reduced to the range of greys, ochres and greens.
The Cubism room gathers different manifestations that
are more or less related, according to circumstances, to
the movement lead by Picasso and Braque, assembling
works of Julio González, Juan Gris, María Blanchard,
Rafael Barradas, Santiago Pelegrín, Pablo Gargallo,
Salvador Dalí and Pablo Picasso.

JUAN GRIS

José Victoriano
González

*He was born in Madrid, in
1887. He died in Boulogne-
surSeine, France, in 1927.
He settled in Paris in
1906, living in the famous
building known as* Bateau-
Lavoir, *where Picasso,
among other Avant-Garde
painters and artists, also
lived. Around 1910, in a
cubist milieu, he did his
first paintings, naturalistic
watercolours very influenced
by Cézanne's work,
followed by others that
were totally cubist. Between
1913 and 1914, he
introduced on his paintings
the* collage *technique.
From the First World War
onwards, he would add
dark shades. Gris describes
the last period of his
evolution as* synthetic,
*with abstract and figurative
compositions coexisting.*

Juan Gris
La guitare devant la mer, 1925
(The Guitar in front of the Sea)
Oil on canvas
53 × 64 cm
Cat. no. 05286

The Guitar in front the Sea belongs to the productive
period between 1915 and 1925, in which Juan Gris
performed his most categorical creations, such as *Jug
and Glass* (1916), *The Bottle of Wine* (1918) or *Still life in
front of the Closet* (1920), all belonging, along with the
mentioned *Guitar in front of the Sea*, to the **Cubism** area.
The initial complexity of the motifs in them, yields to a
stronger will of synthesis, clearing the objects of any
trivial element. A return to the volumetric structure is felt
in some of the works, characteristical in the painter's
output prior to 1913. In this particular canvas, Gris has
chosen the open window as the subject linking his
studio with the nature, with the «plain air» of
impressionist feature.

GARGALLO

Pablo Gargallo

He was born in Maella, Zaragoza, in 1881. He died in Reus, Tarragona, in 1934. In Barcelona he used to patron Els Quatre Gats, meeting artists and painters such as Picasso, Canals or Nonell. He created his first works in cut metal sheet in one of his stays in Paris, in 1907. Back in Barcelona, in 1915, and due to lung problems, he only worked on small size pieces. From 1927 on, he worked in Paris jointly with Julio González, from whom he learned the autogenus welding technique. Certainly, Gargallo has been one of the century's most pioneer sculptors, due to his peculiar way of work, in which volume and space harmoniously coexist.

11

Pablo Gargallo
Masque de Greta Garbo à la meche, 1930
(Greta Garbo's Mask, With A Lock of Hair)
Forged iron
26 × 19 × 12 cm
Cat. no. 00685

There are three versions of this sculpture, in which Gargallo's inspiration were the famous actress' features, although all three differ among them. Its commission to the sculptor by a merchante couple, who wished to obtain the pieces in order to incorporate them in an exhibit about Greta Garbo, seems to be the origin. Gargallo performed several drafts, but the exhibit never did open up and the sketckes got lost. Nevertheless, the artist wanted to carry on the work and modelled by heart the three mentioned versions, with little differences among them. However, all are delicate arabesques of material floating in the space.

Pablo Picasso
Instruments de musique sur une table, 1925
(Musical Instruments on a Table)
Oil on canvas
162 × 204,5 cm
Cat. no. 10615

This huge oil of Picasso, one of the spectacular still lifes
performed at that time by the painter born in Málaga,
bears remarkable resemblances to Salvador Dali's work
Three Figures (1926), which likewise hangs in the
Cubism room. Remarkably, said two compositions, in all
probability carried out independently one from the other
by the respective authors, are complementary and they
reinforce mutually, because of the rotundity of their
volumes and the purity of the motifs represented on
them, as well as to the replacement, also noticeable in
both of them, of the sharp outlines of the initial cubism
by the (more structures) and curvilinear shapes of
that moment.

5

13 14 15

*A*ll along the xxth century, specially during the
period between the two World Wars, a group of
artists and intellectuals, coming from many different places,
came to Paris, turning the French capital into a culturally
exceptional city. This plastic swarm of people was named
Paris School *and replaced Rome as capital of the artistic
world, till the beginning of the Second World War, when the
leadership would move across the Atlantic Ocean, to
New York City.*
Spanish artists had a very important role in this School,
*arriving at the city of the Seine in four successive surges,
from about 1900 up to the Fifties.*
In the room of the Permanent Collection dedicated to the
Paris School, *the works of a group of Spaniards, residing in
the French capital in the inter-war period are shown, some of
these artists are entitled to it in fact by their own right,
(Vázquez Díaz, Dalí, Olivares, Viñes, Manuel Angeles Ortiz,
Cossio or Bores), while others, such as Palencia, Barradas or
Caneja were just passing through Paris, and, even two like
Moreno Villa and Alberto Sánchez, probably never went
to the city of the Seine. Nevertheless, all of them share
the spirit of plastic renewal, characteristic of the bustling
Parisian cultural milieu.*

VAZQUEZ DIAZ
Daniel Vázquez Díaz

He was born in Nerva, Huelva in 1882. He died in Madrid in 1969. In 1906 he settled in Paris where he will remain until 1918, in which time he moved to Madrid, carrying along with him the Cubism doctrin. Somewhat later, he was commissioned to paint a frescos series for the Franciscan Monastery at La Rábida, Huelva, relating Cristopher Columbus' preparations for the Discovery, which work was to become one of his most popular creations. The most outstanding characteristic in his style, is the remarkable geometrical structuring in the compositions, a disposion inherited from the Cubism, which was going to deeply influence the Spanish plastic artists's following generations.

13

Daniel Vázquez Díaz
Alegría del campo vasco (Fuenterrabía), 1920
(Joy of the Basque Countryside (Fuenterrabia)
Oil on canvas
115 × 88 cm
Cat. no. 02211

Vázquez Díaz saw for the first time the Basque landscape in 1906, during his trip to Paris in the same year. From that moment onwards, he would often travel to Fuenterrabia and its outskirts, finding there inspiration for his series of canvases titled *Instants*, that were shown later on in Madrid, in 1947, in the exhibition Room of the *Revista de Occidente*.

These countrysides have nothing in common, although seeming at first glance to the contrary, with the impressionist landscapes, neither in regard to their technique, nor in the final effect. The evanescence of a particular moment is not the objective, but it is the chromatic harmony shown by nature.

D A L Í
....
Salvador Dalí

He was born in Figueras, Gerona, in 1904, and passed away in the same town, in 1989. After became a friend in Madrid with Luis Buñuel and Federico García Lorca, he moved to Paris in 1928, where he met the Surrealist group, getting wholly involved in it. He realized then, together with Luis Buñuel, two very famous movies: An Andalusian dog *and* The Golden Age. *He left the Surrealist movement in 1934, but transmitting it an important legacy: the prospective method, defined by Dalí himself as a paranoic-critical activity. Besides his pictorial production, his drawings are really outstanding, not neglecting his design of jewels, pieces of furniture, fashion design, and cinema, theatre and ballet sceneries.*

....
Salvador Dalí
Paisaje de Cadaqués, 1923
(Cadaqués Landscape)
Oil on canvas
69 × 59 cm
Cat. no. 11128

Dalí spent the summer of 1923 in Cadaqués, reading and painting landscapes like this one, very similar, as much in iconography as in structure and colouring, to another one also performed during the same summer, which main difference lies in its size, somewhat larger than the one we are now discussing.

Dalí was subscribed in those days to the French magazine *Esprit Nouveau*, published by Ozenfant and Le Corbusier, which was a faithful reflect on, among other vanguardist trends, of Purism, revisionist movement in respect to the cubist proposals. Probably, the constructive rigour of said landscape of Cadaqués, comes from the theories spread by this magazine, although the trace of some other painters of a different tendency, as Derain or Sunyer, is also noticeable in this work.

BORES

Francisco Bores

He was born in Madrid, in 1898 and died in Paris in 1972. In the second half of the Twenties, he moved to the French capital where he met Picasso and Juan Gris, painters who did deeply influence his work. He travelled to Provenza in 1930, which trip will mean a change on his style, that, since then onward, will predominate a circular rhythm. Considered already on the Twenties, by the Parisian critic as one of the epoch great painters, his mature style is defined by a sensible mixture of spontaneity and lirism, combined with a compositive structure of cubist origin.

15

Francisco Bores
Coin de chambre, 1925
(Corner of a Room)
Oil on canvas
88 × 64 cm
Cat. no. 5909

Bores himself did assure in some occasion, that the painters he felt closer to, at the time he realized this canvas, 1925, were those whose works echoed, one way or another, the surrealist aesthetics, such as the Spaniards Miró, Cossío or Viñes. In fact, in this *Corner of a Room*, a kind of uncertainty could be felt, perhaps due to the unusual composition perspective or, most likely, the treating of the objects — specially in the clothing piled on the chairs —, that, oddly shaking and twisting, seem to be alive.

*I*n 1924, the Surrealism's leader, the poet André
Breton, published the first manifesto of this literary
and artistical movement, which stated that reason is just an
annoying impediment of creativity development. Starting from
Sigmund Freud's theories, Breton arrived to the conclusion
that, in order to nullify the ties of reason, access to the
subconscious activity must be propitiated by means of the two
main surrealist techniques «par excellence», the automatism
and the reflective disorientation.

In our country, this movement is strongly linked to the
inception of the Avant-Garde prior to the Civil War,
and shows some specific nuances in relation to the
French statements.

This movement, in many of its diverse facets, has been
included in one space of the Permanent Collection, related
mainly to the Spanish artists grouping who used it as way of
expression — Palencia, Rodríguez Luna, Togores, Planells,
Massanet, Oscar Domínguez, González Bernal, Miró,
Marinel·lo, Cristofol or Alberto —, except for a minority
of artists coming from other Countries, but in any case bound
in some way to the reality of Spanish plastics Arts, like
Calder or Arp.

MIRÓ

Joan Miró

He was born in Barcelona, in 1893 and he died in Palma de Mallorca in 1983. In 1919 he travelled for the first time to Paris, in which city, for a long period, he will spend the winter, whereas Montroig will be his customary summer place. He will meet the Avant-Garde in the French capital, where he also became closer friend to Picasso's. He settled in Mallorca in 1941. After the so-called Detailist period, Miró feels the influence of Cubism, with a later evolution towards his own pictorial style, although well linked to Surrealism, where the depicted motifs are enigmatic symbols.

16

Joan Miró
Portrait II, 1938
(Portrait II)
Oil on canvas
162 × 130 cm
Cat. no.08591

Painted by Joan Miró in the period of time when his personal plastic language begins to set, after his closest period to Surrealism (1924-26), this impressive and monumental canvas shows, once again, that surrealist premises will, nevertheless, be always present, in some way, in the painter's work, since, even these canvases do not reproduce images coming from dreams, they are certainly imbued of a kind of special oneiric atmosphere, so disconcerting as enigmatic. Likewise, some graphisms show sometimes up in these works, that although not being performed by automatic writing, they are, however, close to Gesturalism.

DOMÍNGUEZ
....
Oscar Domínguez

He was born in La Laguna, Tenerife, in 1906, and he died in Paris in 1957. He travelled to the French capital in 1927, beginning there his pictorial formation. His first plastic output, already related to Surrealism, are dated in 1929, settling in Paris in that year definitively. His surrealist production in René Magritte's and Salvador Dalí's orbit of creation, will yield between 1938 and 1939 to the so-called Cosmic period, distinguished by a personal style, already secluded, in some way, from Surrealism. At the end of his days, his work shows clearly the influence of the «Picassian» Cubism.

 ....

Oscar Dominguez
Cueva de Guanches, 1935
(Guanche's Cave)
Oil on canvas
81 × 60 cm
Cat. no. 10528

The Oscar Dominguez's production carried out from 1933 on, that is, during his period most identifiable with the orthodox Surrealism, is in a way determined by Salvador Dali's pictorial language, although Dominguez only adopts Dali's way of expression, but in no case the message, as can be appreciated in *Guanche's Cave*, (Guanche: original inhabitant of Canary Islands) which oil belongs to the group of compositions in which, the painter from Canary Island invokes nostalgically his land of birth, as well as in his other works entitled *Butterflies lost in the Mountains* or *Memory of an Island*.

PALENCIA

Benjamín Palencia

He was born in Barrax, Albacete, in 1894. He died in Madrid in 1980. In 1909, he moved to Madrid, where he created, in 1926, the Escuela de Vallecas *(Vallecas School). After a first period with forms very close to Salvador Dalí's around 1925, his style leans towards a kind of more schematic compositions, highly influenced by Cubism. Between 1929 and 1930 he began a new pictorial stage of strong surrealist connotations, following, after the Civil War, a new plastic period, known as* Iberian Fauvism.

 ⑱

Benjamin Palencia
Toros (Tauromaquia), 1933
(Bulls (Bullfighting))
Oil on canvas
79,5 × 95 cm
Cat. no. 06123

A fervent admirer of the Castilian landscape and Alberto Sánchez's fellow in his long walks in the outskirts of Madrid, Benjamín Palencia shows us on his canvas a sober and austere interpretation of the rural world, in which the different motifs of the composition are metamorphosed in biomorphic structures, midway between vegetal and animal kingdom. The painter, sometimes highly close to abstraction, includes in his creations of this period some materials, as unusual as modern, such as sand, soils or ashes. No doubt, *Bulls (Bullfighting)*, is one of his best and most vanguardist creations.

*T*he space mainly devoted to Picasso's Guernica and its preparatory sketches for said canvas, is the axis around which, not only other works belonging to the Spanish AvantGarde prior to the Civil War arearticulated, but also the whole Permanent Collection, since this emblematic painting acts as a link between the mentioned vanguards and the new creations appeared after the war. The Guernica was commissioned to Pablo Picasso by the Spanish Republican Goverment in January 1937, for the Spanish Pavilion at the Paris Internacional World Fair of that year. The painter, touched by the bombing during the Civil War of the Basque town after which the picture is named, realized this huge canvas, with the main topics of the horse and the bull, inspired in a bullfighting phase, and the mother escaping with her dead child on her arms.

Besides the Guernica and its sketches, within this Permanent Collection room, there are also displayed a number of other works related to this picture or to its author. The model of Alberto Sánchez's sculpture The Spanish People Have a Path that Leads to a Star *(1937)*, Picasso's Offering Lady *(1933)* and Salvador Dalí's drawing Premonition of the Civil War *(1935)*, as well as an oil painting by Le Corbusier and two more Picasso's canvases.

Pablo Picasso
Guernica, Paris, May
1st — June 4th, 1937
Oil on canvas
349,3 × 776,6 cm
Cat. no. DE-0050

The first sketch of this impressive canvas is dated on Saturday May 1st of 1937, since Picasso, did work seven days on the preparatory drawings before starting with the final picture composition.

News about the bombardment of the Basque town of Guernica, impulsed him to choose this particular scene, known from the tragic pictures published by the French newspaper *L'Humanité*. In spite of that, the preparatory sketches do not allude specifically to these happenings, but, on the contrary, it represents a manifesto against any kind of barbarity, terror or war in general.

Thus, in the *Guernica* sketches there is nothing identifiable with the Spanish warlike situation: no arms, bombing, soldiers, or planes, but the motifs come from the iconography performed in the author's former works. The only allusive element to the warlike conflict will be the inclusion of a lamp placed in the exact center of the composition, and the lightnings could be the sequel of an explosion.

Alberto
*El pueblo español tiene un camino que conduce
a una estrella*, 1937
*(The Spanish People Have a Path Which Leads
To a Star)*
Plaster
184,5 × 33 × 33 cm
Cat. no. 11424

Alberto, who was commissioned to perform a monumental piece for destination to the Spanish Pavilion at the International World Fair of Paris, in 1937, previously carried out a fully finished model, which constitutes by itself an original piece and which is now exhibited in the Permanent Collection. The final work, shown at the Pavilion entrance, dissapeared on its way back to Spain after closing the Exhibition in 1937, mainly due to the dramatic events happening in those days in our Country, deeply involved in the military conflict.

ALBERTO
....
Alberto Sánchez

Born in Toledo, in 1895, he died in Moscow in 1962. Selfeducated, he created in 1926 together with other painters, the Escuela de Vallecas (Vallecas School). He remained in Moscow from 1938 until his death. After carrying out a group of works directly inspired on nature, he goes through his maturity period, that would last till 1937. From 1955 on, after a long period of full devotion to teaching and stage design, he goes back to sculptural activities, introducing some new materials in his work, such as iron plate and wood pulp, although he will never leave his peculiar style of the Twenties and Thirties.

21
....
Pablo Picasso
La porteuse d'offrande, 1933
(The Offering Lady)
Bronze
220 × 122 × 110 cm
Cat. no. DE-0051

The Offering Lady belongs to the so-called *Boigseloup period* and was one of Picasso's five sculptures the concrete cast of which was exhibited in the Spanish Pavilion at the International World Fair of Paris in 1937. The model is the painter's lover in those years, Marie Thérèse Walter, who was also depicted in some other works of that time.

This piece, although unnoticed to the experts of its author's output, became of such significance to Picasso himself, that even, after his death in 1973, a cast of it was placed over his grave.

* Also entlited by Picasso «La femme au vase» (Woman with a glass)

*W*hen the First World War was over, the international artistic scene sets off on a different tack, known in broad outline as «return to order», which could be defined as a resolute will of replacing the Avant-Garde movements, mainly Cubism and Expressionism, by a new kind of plastic manifestations inspired on classic patterns. This trend will be specially sucessful in Italy and Germany, in which countries there will arise the movements called, respectively, Valori Plastici *(Plastic Values) and* Neue Sachlichkeit *(New Objectivism).*

In Spain, voices asking for this «return to order» were quickly and clearly heard, but in spite of it, like in other countries where this trend was succesful, neither the AvantGarde or the so-called «Arte Nuevo» will follow different ways, but, in most cases, both will appear mixed together.

The Permanent Collection space called Realism *is, in a way, a reflection of the described situation, sometimes coexisting not only very different creations one another, but even, different stylistic trends in the very same work. That space gathers works of Sunyer, Balbuena, Rosario de Velasco, Togores, Arteta, Angeles Santos, Maruja Mallo, Balbino Giner, Ponce de León, López Torres, Dalí, Bores, Manolo Hugué and Daniel González.*

Ángeles Santos
Un mundo, 1929
(A World)
Oil on canvas
290 × 310 cm
Cat. no. 11732

S A N T O S

Ángeles Santos

She was born in Port Bou, Gerona, in 1912. In her childhood, together with her family, she moved respectively to Ripoll, Sevilla and, finally, to Valladolid, in which city she began her plastic production in 1928, and where likewise she performed her most emblematic work, A World (1929). Her painting activity since 1935, when she got married, will stop until 1964, when she takes again her paintbrushes. Ángeles Santos, starting very close to a Surrealism approach, makes later on a turn, on her second pictorial stage, towards more naturalistic positions, where, the performance of her Barcelona urban landscapes series becomes notorious.

The four oil paintings that close this room — Maruja Mallo's *The Fair*, Ponce de León's *Accident*, Balbino Giner's *Godella* and this oil painting by Ángeles Sántos that we now discuss — are all large size, leaving, in a certain way, the Realism, and getting closer to the surrealistic aesthetic, in which some of them fully participate, like, for instance, the emblematic *A World*, where, the Earth planet yields to the painter's plastic and conceptual laws, in a squander of imagination and oniric fantasy. This canvas was painted when the author was almost a teenager, creating a great success in the specialized press. Likewise, due to the excitement originated by this work, some of the most important cultural celebrities of that time, such as Ramón Gómez de la Serna or Federico García Lorca, took a trip to Valladolid, where Ángeles Santos lived at the time, to personally know her.

MALLO

Maruja Mallo

She was born in Tuy, Pontevedra, in 1902. Active participant in Madrid pre-war Avant-Garde trends, she participated in coteries of that time, and gets acquainted with the most famous artists, poets and painters. Her style goes through two clearly distinguished phases in the pre-war period, the first known by its exultated colouring, while in the decade of the Thirties, the most outlined characteristic is precisely, the use of dull and shaded tonalities. Her work in general, might be included in the Hispanic depiction of the Twenties-Thirties, spattered with constant surrealist references.

Maruja Mallo
La verbena, 1927
(The Fair)
Oil on canvas
119 × 166 cm
Cat. no. 01985

It was exactly in 1928 when Maruja Mallo exhibited, in the individual show organized for her by Ortega y Gasset in the *Revista de Occidente* exhibition room, the four oils forming this series devoted to the popular Madrilenian festivities. In all of them, the four pictures on the other hand so close to Surrealism, the painter includes certain characters that act in the way of a linking role, as for instance a kind of peculiar angels or femenin winged figures.

Both the baroque composition and the daring shades utilized, emboss these canvases a strong character of modernity. García Lorca, refering to them, even assured that «I have never seen pictures painted with such an imagination, tender and sensuality as these ones».

PONCE DE LEÓN
....
Alfonso Ponce de León

*He was born in Málaga, in
1900. He died in Madrid,
in 1936. Upon ending his
Fine Arts' studies, he
started getting in touch
with the Avant-Garde
mileu of Madrid. At the
end of the Twenties, he
travelled to Paris. His
campaign on behalf of the
culture, included also other
fields besides the pictorial.
Thus, in 1932 he actively
collaborated in the editing
of the* Arte *magazin,
published by the Sociedad
de Artistas Ibéricos (Iberian
Artists Society).
Furthermore, he designed
costumes and décors for the
university theater* La
Barraca, *making also a
running into the
cinematographic world with
the movie picture «Niños»
(Children) (1931). His
painting production
participates as much in the
Surrealism as in the Magic
Realism.*

Alfonso Ponce de León
Accidente, 1936
(Accident)
Oil on canvas
158 × 188 cm
Cat. no. 00745

Although this scene cannot be considered as strictly
surrealistic but rather closer to the Magic Realism, it
includes however, some oneiric vision connotations,
which feeling is stressed by several factors, like the
strange body position of the protagonist — whose
members get lost between the car headlights and body
— the light illuminatig the injured, that does not seem to
come from the car headlights, and mainly, the odd way of
pointing his forehead with his bloody forefinger the
probably dead protagonist. The strong floodlight, that
shows the outlines and casts misteryous shadows, is
one of the most disturbing elements, giving the canvas
and almost ghostly appearance.

S alvador Dalí began to perform his first paintings
around 1917 and 1918, showing in this initial
period the trace of diverse tendencies.

The so-called Cubist stage *took place approximately between
1922 and 1928, in which period the said influence often
intermingles with motifs coming from the metaphysical
Painting. Within this stage, there is one specially interesting
year. It is in 1925, when the so-called Lorquian period
starts; this denomination is due to the close relationship then
existing between Federico García Lorca and Dalí. Likewise,
in 1925, the painter will perform beautiful paintings of
classical heritage related to the New Objectivism and Valori
Plastici. In 1927, his concern for the Cubism revives,
although this will be a peculiar Cubism, adapted to the
rules of his personality.*

*Later on, in 1928, he settled down in Paris, where he contacts
the surrealist group, performing initially some almost totally
abstract oils. He devotes in 1929 to what was going to
constitute his best known surrealist production, in which the
abstract motifs will yield to an elaborated performance, where
the actual renovation comes from inventing a new exploration
system devising, the paranoic-critical method.*

*The selection of the exhibited works in Dalí's room, perfectly
enlightens everyone of these periods of the painter's production.*

25

Salvador Dali
*Muchacha en la
ventana*, 1925
(Girl at the Window)
Oil on papier mâché
105 × 74,5 cm
Cat. no. 02157

Dali feels in 1925 the influence of the classic legacy recovered by movements like the German *Die Neue Sachlichkeit* or the Italian *Valori Plastici*. Precisely, this classic legacy will create a beautiful series of pictures, the model of which is his sister Ana Maria, being *Girl at the Window* a good example of them. The model herself remembered in a publication of 1949, the long sitting that she had posed for her brother, who patiently depicted on the canvas her curled hair and her bare shoulder, almost always placed near a window, one of his favourite motifs of that time.

 26

Salvador Dali
Arlequín, 1927
(Harlequin)
Oil on canvas
196,5 × 150 cm
Cat. no. 07488

After performing a series of paintings such as the portraits of his sister Ana Maria, Salvador Dalí fully devoted to elaborate an aggregate of works that constitutes his so-called *Cubist period*. For instance, *Harlequin* belongs to this period; the picture was quite unknown till not long ago, although it is not of a minor interest, bearing in mind both its large size and the quality of its performance. Moreover, Dalí's knowledge should be pointed out in combining on the same canvas his admiration for the Avant-Garde — in this case, the Cubism —, and the respect to our painting tradition, as shown by the white folds so close to Zurbarán's.

27

Salvador Dalí
El gran masturbador,
1929
*(The Great
Masturbator)*
Oil on canvas
110 × 150,5 cm
Cat. no. 11140

The putrefaction — perhaps a symbol to Dali of the moral death, the obsolescence of social values at use — is shown in the first place on the famous motif the *Rotten Donkey* which, nevertheless, is not the only one. On the contrary, in Dali's works, the putrefaction also takes possesion of any kind of material, organic or inorganic, mainly on the paintings performed in 1929 and 1930, which happens, for instance, in *The Great Masturbator,* where in addition, the Dalinian fantasies reach their zenith, specially with regard to the motif of the grasshopper that sucks the big metamorphosed figure, which insect frightened the painter since his childhood.

*T*he Civil War was a painful trauma in all aspects
of the Spanish social life, and with regard to the
world of plastic arts, it ruined the different sprouts of the
Avant-Garde that had emerged in the Iberian Peninsula
during the Twenties and Thirties. Thus, the most urgent need
in the decade of the Forties, from an artistic point of view, was
to reshape the national culture. Such initiative would stay in
the hands of private entities, that were either groups or
individuals, like the Academia Breve de la Crítica del Arte,
and the Salones de los Once, both founded by Eugenio D'Ors,
the Escuela de Madrid, some art galleries (Palma, Estilo,
Clan, Buchholz...) or certain groups of painters, such
as Els Vuit, Cobalto, the Escuela de Altamira,
Pórtico or Dau-al-Set.

Unfortunately, in the space of the Permanent Collection called
The Forties, for obvious reasons, such as the non-existance of
funds, there are no representations of those young people who
made up the arising Avant-Garde of that time. Nevertheless,
other more veteran artists are present, but equally sharing the
desire of renovation, such as José Caballero or Angel Ferrant,
Picasso or Granell and Wildfredo Lam, the latter although
not born in Spanish territory, had become deeply involved
with the plastic realities of our Country.

FERRANT
....
Angel Ferrant

He was born in Madrid, in
1890, and he died in the
same city, in 1961. Active
member of the Avant-
Garde prior to the Civil
War, he created in 1949 his
first Mobiles, of which he
will always exclude the
movement by means of an
engine, although his
interest for the movement
itself was already shown in
previous works. Likewise,
he was interested, as plastic
elements, in the found
objects, *(wire, cork, shells,*
stones or metal sticks), that
he manipulated to
transform them into
sculptures or reliefs.
Starting from the surrealist
aesthetic, he creates two
fundamental kind of pieces,
those performed on stone —
generally figuratives — and
others of an abstract nature
in which the main interest
is focused on the inclusion
of movement.

28 ....
Angel Ferrant
Estático cambiante, 1953
(Changing Static)
Birch wood, steel plates.
Shaft: Iron foundry
274,5 × 127,5 × 126,5 cm
Cat. no. 01146

Ferrant's works exhibited in the Permanent Collection,
show the influence of the Avant-Garde experiences
undergone by its author in his Barcelona stage, before
settling down in Madrid. In spite that he destroyed the
pieces performed in Barcelona around 1932 — which was
a quite usual habit of Ferrant in moments of subjective
dissatisfaction with his own work —, the surrealistic and
abstract tendency of the mentioned objects still exists in
the new works performed in Madrid. The sculptor was
commissioned to produce the mobil *Changing Static* by
Fernández del Amo, while he was Director of the former
«Museo Español de Arte Contemporáneo», bound for
said Center and it is one of his most successful
creations in the field of sculpture in motion.

29

Pablo Picasso
Monument aux espagnols morts pour la France,
1946-1947
(Monument to the Spaniards killed fighting for France)
Oil on canvas
195 × 130 cm
Cat. no. 11273

Picasso, worried by the events happening during the
Second World War, shows in his canvases his state of
mind. Once the war was over, in 1945, he performed also
the famous oil painting entitled *The Ossuary*, which was
an accurate reflection of the catastrophe that had
recently happened. *The Monument to the Spaniards
killed fighting for France*, should be considered along
this same line; this picture was donated by the French
Governement to the Spanish State, in 1990, and with
which Picasso participated, together with the mentioned
The Ossuary, in the «Arte y Resistencia» exhibition,
inagurated in the Modern Art Museum of Paris in 1946.
Curiosly, this work is dated by its author subsequent to
the mentioned exhibition, perharps because Picasso
himself might have touched it up after the show.

32
33
31
11
30
12

*A*ccording to Gillo Dorfles, the adjective
informal — the word Informalism derives from it
— implies an idea of rebelliousness against preconceived
elements, proposing the annulment of any kind of formal and
conceptual structure. This trend, which images will no longer
come from the external reality but from the artist's own self,
will be characterized by the great importance bestowed by its
followers to the physical act of painting, as well as for the
preponderant rôle of the utilized materials, that are sometimes
totally unusual, like Millare's burlaps or Rivera's wire mats.
The Spanish Informalism developed mainly in two focal
points: Madrid and Catalonia; Barcelona was precisely the
land where this kind of performances were firstly seen, thanks
to a group of painters who, always individually, followed the
movement. However, in Madrid, the Informalism materialized
later on, structuring by means of associations, of which,
the most significative was El Paso.
In the rooms that the Permanent Collection has devoted to
this trend, it is possible to contemplate its different forms,
from the Catalonian artist's works — Tàpies, Cuixart,
Guinovart — up to the sober creations arisen around the
members of the group El Paso — Millares, Saura, Rivera,
Serrano, Feito, Canogar, Chirino, Viola — not forgetting other
authors' performances, also attached to Informalism, such as
Chillida, Lucio Muñoz, Torner, Rueda, Salvador Victoria,
Ràfols Casamada, Zóbel, Mompó, Guerrero or
Esteban Vicente.

TÀPIES

Antoni Tàpies

He was born in Barcelona, in 1923. Together with Joan Brossa, he founded in 1948 the magazine and the group Dau al Set, in which Cuixart, Tharrata, Ponç and Arnau Puig did also participate. In 1970 he performed his first sculptures. His work starts off from the surrealist aesthetic to end in a special typology of Informalism, in which material, monochrome and wall-scrapping, all related, in a way, to the Zen philosophy, reach an outstanding importance. Tàpies has been winner of very important international awards, his performance has been acknowledged in exibitions organized by some of the most important Museums. He has also participated in the literature field, publishing works and statements such as Art's performance (1970), Letters to Theresa (1974) or Personal Memory (1978).

30

Antoni Tàpies
Superposició de matéria grisa, 1961
(Superposition of Grey Material)
Mixed media on canvas
197 × 263 cm
Cat. no. 10532

Tàpies, who between 1945 and 1947 already appeared deeply interested on materials, developed again this kind of composition approximately from 1954 till 1963, partly stimulated by watching in Paris Dubuffet's work, and, mainly, Fautrier's, who in 1950 had already started to perform his series devoted to *boxes* and *objects*. In *Painting* (1955), also exhibited in the Informalism room, the topic by excellence of this moment, the wall, starts to show in the different manipulations realized on the canvas surface — incisions, scratches... —, but where really the said topic forcefully arises, is, however, in the work we comment now, the magnificent composition entitled *Superposition on Grey Material*.

CHILLIDA

Eduardo Chillida

He was born in San Sebastián, in 1924. Since 1958, when, for the first time, he individually exhibited in the Galería Clan, in Madrid, shows of his work have continuously suceeded all over the world, while his production was displayed at important museums like the Guggenheim in New York City. His sculptures start from a series of figurative pieces that very soon, about 1950, are replaced by already abstract creations. His preferred materials, formed either by dynamic graphics or in heavy architectural bulk, are concrete, steel, alabaster and, mainly, iron. Eduardo Chillida has also performed notorious works in the engraving and printing fields.

31

Eduardo Chillida
Espíritu de los pájaros I, 1953
(The Spirit of the Birds I)
Forged iron and stone
56 × 92,5 × 42,5 cm
Cat. no. 01337

Eduardo Chillida, at the end of Forties decade, already perfomed pieces as successful, from the constructive point of view, as his *Busts* in bronze, in which, his very Avant-Garde spatial concept, perfectly coexists with certain reminiscences of the archaic Greek statuary. However, this same wisdom with which the sculptor knows how to combine the fullness and the void, shows fully in works like this *Spirit of the Birds I*, one of his first iron works, which material will be his favourite from the beginning of the Fifties up to 1960, and from this date on, it will be also utilized with a certain frequency.

S A U R A

Antonio Saura

*He was born in Huesca in
1930. He moved in 1953
to Paris, where he stayed
till 1955, participating
during some time in the
activities of the surrealist
group. Already in Madrid
in 1957, he decisively
contributes to the creation
of the El Paso group, an
actual melting pot where
the informalist renovation
was created, through the
inclusion of gesture
techniques of the
international scene. Starting
from an initial period that
was very influenced by the
Surrealism, his work tends
later on to the Informalism
of expressionist nature,
structured around
compositions generally
solved by means of white
and black tones, in which
one feels the great classic
masters mark, such as
Rembrandt, Goya or
El Greco.*

Antonio Saura
Grito Nº 7, 1959
(Scream nº 7)
Oil on canvas
250 × 200 cm
Cat. no. D-0036

The year of foundation of the group *El Paso*, Antonio
Saura starts to perform his famous *Crucifixions* series,
in which some critics think to see a deep mystic sense,
while some others were scandalized, since they
supposed that the painter meant thereby to make a
mock of the Catholic religion. The twisted crucified of
these pictures are not, however, neither blasphemeous
nor mystic, only meaning, according to the author, to
offer the image of a man alone and absurdly hanged on
a cross facing a threatening universe. A result of Saura's
violent and gestural plastic language, always between
the abstract and the figurative, is this *Scream n⁰ 7*, a
mixture of crucifixion and femenin nude that,
exasperated and sorrowful, raises its arms to heaven
in a hopeless clamour.

MILLARES

Manuel Millares

He was born in Las Palmas de Gran Canaria, in 1926. He died in Madrid, in 1972. In 1950 he collaborated in the foundation of the **LADAC** *group (The Archers of the Contemporary Art). In 1957 he participated in the creation and subsequent development of* El Paso *group. One year later, in 1958, he published his text* Homunculus in the current Painting *in the* Papeles de Son Armadams, *a magazine devoted to the referred group* El Paso. *His first performances, the famous Canary Pictographies, are influenced by the study on the Guanche culture. Later on, he became interested in the surface and texture of the supports, which will determine his mature style, always within the Informalism limits.*

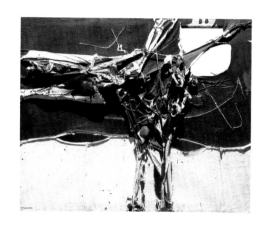

33 ....

Manuel Millares
Cuadro 173, 1962
(Painting 173)
Mixed media on burlap
130 × 163 cm
Cat. no. 10583

Manuel Millares, who was at the beginning linked to the Canary Islands aboriginal iconography, began to turn the burlap into the protagonist of his works around 1953. After settling in Madrid in 1955, coming from his home town, Las Palmas de Gran Canaria, burlap is gaining more solidity and volume, until it forms a kind of torn bodies called by Millares himself *homúnculos*. Colour — or rather, its nearly total absence — contributes to the general feeling of deep drama, what is clearly shown in works like this *Painting 173*.

*B*etween 1919 and 1922, when he had already
assimilated the Cubism and the Fauvism, Miró
carried out a series of compositions of which the most
significant testimony is The Farm (1922), while the later
development of his work known as surrealist, happens from
1923 to 1929, although the painter kept always his
independence with regard to groups and ideologies. About
1929-1930, due to a crisis that leads him to reconsider his
activity as a painter, he mainly devoted himself to perform
collages and a series of constructions in relief. His tormented
monsters will appear in 1934 which will yield in 1938,
to the consolidation of his plastic vocabulary, taking
it up in the future once again.

His last stage starts from approximately 1962 until his death,
in 1983, and, precisely, the works that make up the room
Miró in the Seventies, belong to that stage. The artist, far
from loosing his energy with age, seems to recover his vigour,
which is reflected in his last performances, where, besides
gesturallity and strength, he also enlarges the format of his
works. Specifically, there are sixteen pieces included in
this Permanent Collection, of which, eleven are paintings
and the other five, sculptures.

34

Joan Miró
Paysage, 1976
(Landscape)
Oil on canvas
130 × 194,5 cm
Cat. no. 08877

The main motifs of the Mironian iconography are those alluding the firmament and the heavenly bodies: the stars, the constellations, the sun and the moon. The sun is a big red balloon suspended on heaven and generally flat. Conversly, the moon is always depicted in last quarter or in first quarter, everlasting blue. Constellations and stars are the expression of a spiritual universe, that already got rid of the ballast of material. As shown in this *Landscape*, the most usual kind of star is that formed by several very thin lines that coincide and interlace in the middle, although there also exists other kind of stars, some small circles that sometimes are interconnected forming constellations, which perhaps is inspired on the romantic murals in the Catalonian Pyrenees, so dear to Miró.

35

Joan Miró
Sin título I, 1973
(Untitled I)
Oil on canvas
195 × 130 cm
Cat. no. 08882

Red and blue are the base of Miró's chromatic repertory. Red is energy and health, is the incarnation of straightness, of the tangible, of the sun, of birds, of sexual organs and, sometimes also, of the land over which all human being are settled. Blue usually shapes huge portions that make up the background of the

picture, and over them, the magic motifs created by the
author. Nevertheless, occasionally, blue paint condenses
in isolated and mysterious spots, absolute protagonists
of the scene, in unknown but placid spaces, from where,
worry and anxiety have been totally banished, as felt in
this canvas, *Untitled I*.

Joan Miró
Horloge du vent, 1967
(Wind Clock)
Bronze
49,5 × 29,5 × 16 cm
Cat. no. 10541

Miró's interest in three-dimensional pieces goes back to
1931, when he performed his first sculpture-object,
entitled *Man and Woman*. In 1944, together with Llorens
Artigas, he carried out his initial pottery work, and in the
second half of the Sixties, about 1966-67, he began to
forge works on bronze, recovering, in a way, the spirit of
his objects in the surrealist stage.

The process of the latter years sculptures begins with
the gathering of any kind of scrap elements, found at
random, which Miró later on manipulates and assembles.
Before carrying out the piece to its final material, bronze,
the artist works on it again, impressing strokes or prints
on the wax. Some of the most beautiful of these
sculptures, always between humour and uneasiness, are
shown in the **Miró in the Seventies** room, like this *Wind
Clock*, that actually is a hatbox pierced by a wood spoon.

14

39 38 37

*T*he Constructive term, comparable to the sense Constructive Art, has never been clearly defined, as it is being used in most cases as a synonim of Geometric Abstraction. However, it can be stated that actual specifity of Constructivism lies in the fact of being understood as an artistic trend based on reflexion and investigation, as opposed to those other trends conceived as a product of improvisation and even by means of automatism, as it happens in the surrealist manifestations and even in the Informalism.

Spain joined belatedly the Geometric Abstraction, in the Fifties. While the Informal Art reaped its best results, a series of constructivist rashes also arised, though more timidly, among whose main cultivators there are precisely the four names — one group and three individual — who are included in the Permanent Collection room named Constructive Art: Jorge de Oteiza, Equipo 57, Pablo Palazuelo and Eusebio Sempere.

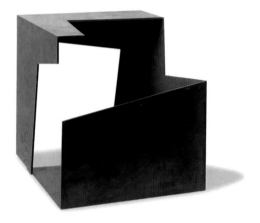

He was born in Orio, Guipúzcoa in 1908. Involved in a constant controversy because of his always radical and polemic ideas, he writes between 1956 and 1957 his Experimental Purpose, *in which volume he shows his theoretical posits about the experimentation with the void and the* unoccupied space. *His plastic evolution goes back to 1935, when he performed a series of pieces with found objects. About 1950, he shows partly Henry Moore's influence in his solid forms perforated in its core. Finally, on his last production years, he leans towards the experimental Constructivism, thus carrying out his spatial theories.*

Jorge de Oteiza
Caja metafísica, 1958
(Metaphysical Box)
Iron
30 × 32,5 × 30 cm
Cat. no. 08717

From a formal point of view, Oteiza, although having used sometimes the sphere, prefers the cube as a basic abstract element to realize his plastic experimentation, as in his opinion, said geometric figure symbolizes the metaphysical relationship between man and cosmos. The void — already appraised by the cubist sculptors — thanks to the process named by the sculptor himself like *unoccupied space*, goes from being a component of the three-dimensional work to become an essential element of it, in the invigorating agent that gives sense to the piece. All this can be appreciated in the group of performances exhibited in the space **Constructive Art** of the Permanent Collection, and mainly in the *Metaphysical Box*, work belonging to the stylistic maturity period of its author.

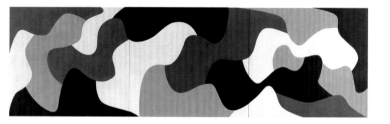

J. Cuenca, A. Duarte, J.
Duarte, A. Ibarrola and
J. Serrano

Juan Cuenca was born in
Puente Genil, Córdoba, in
1934. Angel Duarte, in
Aldeanueva del Camino,
Cáceres, in 1930. José
Duarte, in Córdoba in
1928. Agustín Ibarrola, in
Bilbao, in 1930. Juan
Serrano, in Córdoba, in
1929. Equipo 57 *starts as*
such a group in the summer
of 1957, and its activity is
directly inspired in the
artistic practice of the
sculptor Jorge de Oteiza.
Their plastic performances
are inseparable from their
theorical researches, which
are brought together in a
series of works known, in a
generic way, as Manifestos
about the plastic space
interactivity. In their
painting stage, always
based on the constructive
abstraction, four stages are
to be distinguished and, in
the last one, there are
noticed some concomitancces
with the optical-kinetic Art.

Equipo 57
Triptico, 1960
(Tryptic)
Acrylic on tablex
122 × 411 cm
Cat. no. 01854

This picture, *Tryptic*, could be placed in the third of the
three periods in which the *Equipo 57* is structured,
stage in which, the outlines delimiting the different
coloured surfaces, have already softened their
contours, while the motifs are getting smaller, also
repeating themselves with a certain cadence. The
large size of this picture — one of the largest
performed by its authors — should be emphasized,
and also the fact of the exclusive use in its
performance of grey and black shades. Both
circumstances — the oblong and monumental format
and the resolution of the composition by means of the
grisaille — might be an *Equipo 57*'s veiled homage to
Picasso's *Guernica*.

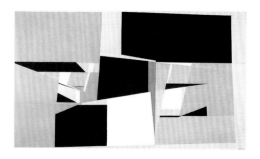

PALAZUELO
....
Pablo Palazuelo

He was born in Madrid in 1916. He studied in Oxford and later on, in 1948, he travelled to Paris, where most of his plastic development took place. His first performances date from 1940, in which period he shows both the neocubist influence and the mark of Klee's, Mondrian's or Kandisky's work. From 1946 on, his production becomes fully abstract, forming part of the Constructivism. His first three-dimensional performances date from 1954, translating to those sculptures the researches previously carried out on canvas.

39
....
Pablo Palazuelo
Otoños, 1952
(Falls)
Oil on canvas
82 × 143 cm
Cat. no. 08115

Palazuelo, who was very much influenced at his early stage by Paul Klee's work, found however very soon his own way in the field of Constructivism, which he will leave behind too later on, although the stamp of this movement will be always felt in his creations. When he performed *Falls* in 1952, lyrism and delicacy that will characterize his later works are already present, in spite of the strict structuring of the geometric motifs that form said canvas. The shade chosen here is likewise austere — perhaps inspired in the Cubism — and it is perfectly in agreement with the painter's preferences in those years, where the black shades are in contrast with the gamut of ochres, tinged in turn by the presence of gray and white pigments.

*A*ssembled under the epigraph Proposals, several
spaces have been articulated, that contrast deeply
with the rest of the rooms of the Collection. It is an
innovatory museological conception, that deliberately avoids
any kind of, either chronological or thematic, disposition, since
the principal aim is the individual assessment of the displayed
works, shown here as individual pieces, the only link of which
could be their acknowledged representativeness within the
context of the present artistic scene.

The first of these works belongs to the sculptor Julio Lopéz
Hernandez, one of the most outstanding members of Group
of Madrilenian realist, coming next a huge sculpture and
eleven collages of Eduardo Chillida's. Lucio Fontana's seven
performances are located in the third of these areas, whereas
the fourth one is devoted to the respective works of Picasso,
Bacon, Matta, Miquel Navarro and Tony Cragg. The next
room houses Tapiès, Newman, Bleckner, Scully, Kapoor and
Susana Solano various works, whereas two beautiful works of
Ellsworth Kelly's and Jesús Rafael Soto's, share another space,
which act as a kind of anteroom of the space devoted to
Schnabel. Finally, the Spanish painting of authors such as
Arroyo, Gordillo or Equipo Cronica, precedes the last two
Proposals, Bruce Nauman's and Dan Flavin's rooms.

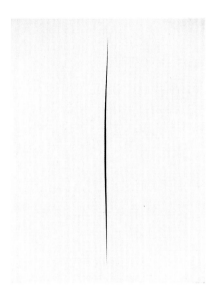

F O N T A N A
....
Lucio Fontana

*He was born in Rosario de
Santa Fé, Argentina, in
1899. He died in the
Italian town of Comabbio,
in 1968. In 1934 he was a
member of the* Italian
Abstract *group, and in
1935 he joined other
vanguardist grouping,*
Abstraction-Crèation, *of
Paris, signing also on that
year, the first collective
exhibit manifesto of «Arte
Astratta Italiana». From
1947 on, he writes his*
Spatials Manifestos. *On
his sculptural activity
beginnings, his work will
show Alexander
Archipenko's influence.
However, the main concern
of his mature style will be
the threedimensional space
incorporation on the
painting, which he will
obtain by perforating or
slashing the bare, pigment
free canvas.*

....
Lucio Fontana
Concetto spaziale. Attesa, 1960
(Spatial Concept. The Wait)
Acrylic on canvas
116 × 89 cm
Cat. no. 11743

Lucio Fontana's great concern in finding the synthesis of
all physical elements — «colour, sound, movement, space,
in a unit at the same time ideal and material» — in the
artistic creation, as well as his strong determination to
abolish the limits between painting and sculpture, is
shown in works like this *Spatial Concept. The Wait* which
forms, together with the other monochrome and
perforated compositions that make up this room of The
Collection, a kind of involving and peculiar area in which
the spectator feels as belonging to the work, involved in
that magic and proper space which said work shapes.

41 ....

Pablo Picasso
El pintor y la modelo, 1963
(Painter and Model)
Oil on canvas
130 × 195 cm
Cat. no. 02035

This canvas, belonging to the *Painter and Model* series,
was acquired, together with two others also exhibited in
this room and belonging to the mentioned series, to be
exhibited in the Spanish Pavilion of the 1966
International World Fair of New York City. The depicted
subject, already performed by the artist in the last years
of the Twenties, will reach its magnificence peak just in
the time that the picture we comment now was
performed, during the Sixties. After his marriage with
Jacqueline Roque in 1961, Picasso begins to paint
almost compulsively, performing a multitude of paintings
which model is usually Jacqueline. Sometimes there are
not just pictures, but even dainty and expressive
sculptures or attractive ceramic plates. This oil lies
on that context, in which the painter, once again,
pays homage to his wife and muse.

NEWMAN

Barnett Newman

He was born in New York City, in 1905, passing away in same city, in 1970. After participating in the Federal Arts Project, *he collaborated in the foundation of the artistic school* Subjects for the Artist, *making compatible as well, his painting devotion with his activity as university professor. In 1968 he travelled to Barcelona interested in knowing Gaudí's work. Considered as the most influential American artist of the Sixties, he performes an output that goes through the diverse stages of the abstract Expressionism and which, in spite of its apparent simplicity, bears manifold meanings, which are directly corresponded with its author's feelings and experiences.*

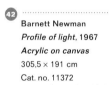

42
....
Barnett Newman
Profile of light, 1967
Acrylic on canvas
305,5 × 191 cm
Cat. no. 11372

Newman, finding inspiration at first in the triangles, rectangles and circles used by the Russian constructivists and the Dutch movement *De Stijl*, however, he goes soon beyond any external influence and creates a style, or better, his absolutely own poetics. *Profile of light* is an enigmatic and huge painting made up by three vertical colour bands which shades, on basis of white and ultramarine blue, interfer between themselves, although being absolutely independent one from other, producing a luminosity as deep as mysterious. This painting, contemplated from a close distance — as Newman recommended to be done with all his works — seems to go beyond its own limits, creating a kind of surrounding space that emanates from itself.

KELLY

Ellsworth Kelly

He was born in Newburgh, New York, in 1923. In 1948 he travelled to Paris, where he will stay until 1954, painting during his first months of his stay in the French capital, a kind of portraits influenced by Picasso, the Byzantine Art and the Roman Art, styles on which he had been interested since his student days in the U.S. Author as much of paintings as of sculptures and reliefs, he has been considered as one of the most genuin followers of Mondrian's Neoplasticism. Although developing a kind of performances near, in a way, to the geometric abstraction, his compositions, of large octogonal plans and vibrant colours, are usually inspired in organic forms.

Ellsworth Kelly
Concorde, 1958
Oil on canvas
193 × 147 cm
Cat. no. 11487

Ellsworth Kelly's *Concorde*, was performed just four years after its author's left Europe — he had stayed in Paris from 1948 until 1954 — to settle back in The United States, his native land. In the French capital city, Kelly had had the chance of meeting Vantongerloo, a member of Dutch Neoplasticism, and also with Jean Arp. From both of them he takes out the basis of what will be his future style, in which the minimalist aesthetics will also have to do definitively. Between 1959 and 1961, he performed a group of canvases which main figure is usually an irregular polyhedrom that interferes in certain points in the edges of a rectangular ground. *Concorde*, although performed a year before, in 1958, is a foretaste of that series, inspired, as it usually happens in the painter's work, in shapes created by the nature.

MOVEMENTS

SCHOOLS

GROUPS

TRENDS

LEXICON

Grands-Agustins studio. Picasso with
Joaquin Peinado. Hernando Viñes with
other people.
Vaclav Chochola photograph (Praga).

MOVEMENTS, SCHOOLS, GROUPS AND TRENDS

Abstraction. Artistic trend not based in the resemblance between the depicted motif and the visual image but in the adequate colour and distribution of forms, letting the author free to express his feelings and experiences.

Academia breve de la Critica del Arte. Association created in 1941, under Eugenio D'Ors' management with the aim, stated in its foundational **Proclama** (Manifesto), of divulging in the postwar Madrid «some pages of the universal contemporary art», as well as with the purpose of organizing future exhibitions called «Salones de los Once» (Halls of the Eleven) that took place in the successive occasions in the gallery Biosca, in Madrid. Members of the *Academia Breve* were artists, architects, art critics, art gallery owners, professors, members of the diplomatic corps and society men.

Constructivism. An abstract movement arisen in Russia about 1913, around Vladimir Tatlin, who defended the construction supremacy over the representation and functionality of the artistic work, integrated into the social needs. The members of this movement, inspired in the Cubism, performed a series of geometric compositions that will influence both in later pictorial performances and in the industrial design. This influence extended to a great part of the geometric painting, even using the term Constructivism as a qualifier for several movements arisen in the Fifties and Sixties.

Constructivism Abstraction. See **Constructivism**.

Cubism. Artistic movement created about 1907 by Pablo Picasso and Georges Braque, that, with a strong will of rigorism, tries to build the volume by means of the coloured surface, limiting the nature to elemental geometric shapes and depicting the objects by its permanent formal qualities. Its immediate precedent is the later work of the French painter Paul Cèzanne. This movement went through three fundamental stages, the *analytic* Cubism (1908-1911), in which an exhaustive analysis of the depicted motif is carried out; the *hermetic* Cubism (1911), of a marked tendency towards abstraction; and the *synthetic* Cubism (1912-1914), in which an iconographic selection is introduced to help legibility of the motif. Cubism would become one of the most important movements of the XXth century, determining a great part of later trends.

Dadaism. Artistic trend arisen — as an intelectual attitude — in 1916, led by the Romanian Tristan Tzara. Participants of this trend were painters, sculptors and poets who, from different places of Europe, reacted against the irrationality and barbarity that the First World War represented by rejecting the traditional values, as much in the field of arts as in life in general. Their claim for freedom led them to choose new artistic ways such as the *ready-made* or the *collage*. Dada, term that names the movement, was chosen by its founder opening at random a dictionary, what shows the dadaist phylosophy in returning the social absurd with the followers personal absurd.

Dau al Set. Association sprouted in Barcelona in 1948 around the publication equally named, and formed by intelectuals and artists such as Joan Brossa, Arnau Puig, Antoni Tàpies, Modest Cuixart, Joan Josep Tharrats or Joan Ponç. **Dau al Set**, inspired in the Surrealism and Dadaism, was one of the most outstanding groups of the post-Civil War Spanish Avant-Garde.

Ecole de Paris. (Paris School) Denomination used to name a group of artists, mainly Europeans, who made of the French capital their usual workplace and home, mainly during the between-wars period till the beginning of the Second World War, when the Avant-Garde scene moved to New York City. Of a great importance for the birth of many artistic movements, its members are only linked by the fact of living in the town that names the said School.

El Paso. Artistic association formed in Madrid in 1957, that meant the informalist poetics arrival to Spain, being the link between the international avant-garde trends and the Spanish artists new generations. Among its members are Rafael Canogar, Antonio Saura, Manuel Millares,

Manuel Rivera, Martín Chirino, Manuel Viola, Luis Feito and Pablo Serrano.

Escuela de Altamira. (Altamira School) Artistic experience that, from 1948, brought together a group of painters and critics, by initiative of the German painter Mathias Goeritz. Of a strong cosmopolitan character, aided to the cultural exchange between national Avant-Garde artists and some outstanding international painters and sculptors.

Escuela de Madrid. (Madrid School) A painters association that arose on the occasion of the «Joven Escuela de Madrid» exhibit, held in the Buchholz Gallery in 1945. Based on the artistic apprenticeship of painters such as Solana, Vázquez Díaz and Palencia, the new group rejected the doctrine of the Escuela de Bellas Artes de San Fernando, and seeked to reinforce the Spanish after-war art by means of a new landscape interpretation. Among its main members are Cirilo Martínez Novillo, Alvaro Delgado, Francisco Arias, Juan Manuel Díaz Caneja, Juan Guillermo, Agustín Redondela, Gregorio del Olmo and Francisco José.

Escuela de Vallecas. (Vallecas School) Artistic experience developed in Madrid since 1927 by the painter Benjamín Palencia

and the sculptor Alberto Sanchéz, that was joined later on by other artists such as Juan Manuel Díaz Caneja, Maruja Mallo, José Bergamin, Rafael Alberti or Federico García Lorca, among others, with the aim of revitalizing the Spanish artistic scene, emulating the experiences carried out in Paris. Its name comes from the said artists's choice of Vallecas landscapes as agglutinative element of their plastic experiences. It is also known as *Primera Escuela de Vallecas* (First Vallecas School).

Expressionism. Artistic trend in which the expression of the artist's internal experiences prevails against the external world representation. It is used currently in the plastic arts field, to name a specific artistic movement developed at the beginning of the XXth century, mainly in Germany and agglutinated around two groups, *Die Brucke* (The Bridge) (1905-1913), and *Der blaue Reiter* (The blue Knight), arisen in 1911. Likewise, in 1918 a third also German expressionist appearance is born, personified by the group named *Neue Sachlichkeit* (New Objectivity).

Fauvism. Pictorial movement appeared in

Paris in 1905, under Henri Matisse's leadership, who gathered around himself a number of painters — Derain, Vlaminck, Van Dongen...— dubbed by the critic Louis Vauxcelles as *Les Fauves* (The Beasts). Its main characteristic is the free use of colour and the violence of brushstrokes as well as the fact that in their art works, the external world is no longer depicted but the inner feelings, the artist's psychological experiences.

Futurism. Movement of artistic agitation arisen in Italy in 1909, when the poet Marinetti's *Manifesto* was published, propounding as supreme values the dynamism of the modern way of life and the cult of the machine, against the respect for tradition. Regarding the plastic arts, the pointillist brushstroke becomes widely used, while colour gets close to the used by expressionist painters, and relation between form and space comes directly from Cubism. Its most outstanding performers are Umberto Boccioni, Giacomo Balla, Carlo Carrá and Gino Severini.

Geometric Abstraction. Abstraction variety in which, conversely to the so-called lyric abstraction or of expressive nature, there is an evident prevail of lines, geometric forms and, in most cases, of flat colours.

Grupo LADAC. (The Archers of the Contemporary Art). Group of artists from the Canary Islands gathered around the group's theorist, Eduardo Westerdahl. They made their debut in the Syra Gallery, Barcelona, in 1951. LADAC members were Felo Monzón, Juan Ismael, José Julio and Manuel Millares, who, in their respective works, combined the respect for their native culture with the international Avant-Garde teaching.

Grupo Pórtico. (Pórtico Group) Artist association arisen in Zaragoza in 1947. It was formed mainly by the painters Eloy Laguardia, Santiago Lagunas and Fermin Aguayo, who carried out the first abstract compositions performed in the Spanish artistic scene of that time.

Informalism. Abstract trend arisen from the Second World War on in France, partially as a reaction against the American abstract Expressionism. Its main characteristic is the total absence of formal structure, excluding even the geometric forms, and its concern for spots, material, texture and the caligraphyc stroke as direct expressions of the painter's self. Said trend was introduced in Spain

mainly by Antoni Tàpies, in Barcelona, and by *El Paso* in Madrid.

LADAC.
See **LADAC Group.**

Los Arqueros del Arte Contemporáneo.
See **LADAC Group.**

Magic Realism.
See **Neue Sachlichkeit.**

Neoplasticism. Dutch movement originated in 1917 simultaneously as its sopkesmagazine, *De Stijl*, always stimulated by the painter Piet Mondrian. Inspired in Cubism, the Neoplasticism upholds the sole use of right angle and reduces the chromatism to six varieties, the three primary colours — blue, red and yellow — and the three «no-colours» — white, black and grey —. It extended to other fields off the pictorial, mainly towards architecture, sculpture and industrial design.

Neue Sachlichkeit. (New Objectivity) Movement of realist origin born in Germany about 1925, with followers such as Grosz, Otto Dix, Karl Hubbuch, Rudolf Schlichter, Anton Räderscheidt, Carl Grossberg or Christian Schad. Based on the conviction of social task of the art, its followers made a sour criticism of the habits of Germany on the Twenties. Actually, it grouped two specific arieties, the so-called *Neue Sachlichkeit*, term xtended to the whole movement, characterized y its most radical roposals, and the *Magic Realism*, faction closer to urrealism named after the omonymous book ublished by Franz Roh in 925.

New Objectivity.
See **Neue Sachlichkeit.**

Orfism. Term coined by Guillaume Apolinaiire in 912 to designate Robert Delaunay's artistic output. This movement formally coincides with Cubism, but nlike it, it includes colour in its compositions and attaches great importance o light, linking in a way with Impressionism. Sonia Delaunay and Frantisek Kupka also belonged to it. Robert Delaunay's orfist performances may be considered, together with andisky's works, as the Xth century first abstract realizations.

Pintura metafisica.
See **Pittura metafisica.**

Pittura metafisica. (Metaphysical Painting) rtistic trend created in Italy by Giorgio de Chirico 1917 in which Carlo Carrà and Giorgio Morandi participated too. Arisen as a reaction against the futurist dynamism, it takes he classic peace and serenity as leitmotiv.

Ideologically connected with philosophical trends which greatest concern lies on the fugacity of the existence, its followers identify beauty with the patina that time provides to objects. Most usual subjects are mainly desolate and enigmatic urban landscapes, very close to the surrealist oneiric visions.

Pórtico.
See **Grupo Pórtico.**

Primera Escuela de Vallecas.
See **Escuela de Vallecas.**

Realism. Term that defines those aesthetic attitudes or tendencies which try to reproduce accurately the reality, sometimes adding a personal opinion of the artist himself, about the depicted reality.

Salones de los Once.
See **Academia Breve de la Crítica del Arte.**

Segunda Escuela de Vallecas. (Second Vallecas School) Artistic experience happened in Madrid shortly after the Civil War which was the prolongation of the so-called *Escuela de Vallecas* or *Primera Escuela de Vallecas*, and also arisen in Madrid in the Twenties. This *Segunda Escuela de Vallecas*, agglutined around Benjamin Palencia,

was formed by the painters Luis Castellanos, Francisco San José, Alvaro Delgado, Gregorio del Olmo y Carlos Pascual de Lara. It did not last long and its objectives were focused on the renewal of the national artistic scene with Vallecas landscape as starting point.

Stijl, De.
See **Neoplasticism.**

Surrealism. Literary and artistic trend arisen in 1924 under the writer and poet André Breton's leadership. Its theorical ideology, starting from Sigmund Freud's psychoanalitic findings, defends the free access to the subconscious images, without the rational controls, utilizing two main procedures that constitute the two emblematic surrealist techniques: the *automatism* and the *reflexive disorientation*. Surrealists practised also creative games such as the *exquisite corpse*. In the movement core there were made two representation varieties: the *objective line*, in which, works that follow reality forms participate, and the *antiobjective line*, in which more or less abstract realizations not reproducing naturals forms are comprised.

Valori Plactici. (Plastic Values) Artistic trend arisen in Rome in 1918,

around the homonymous
magazin, with the aim to
carry out the one known as
«return to order», that is,
the replacement of avant-
garde movements, mainly
Cubism and
Expressionism, by a new
kind of plastic
manifestations inspired in
classic patrons. In 1922,
the group changed its
name, being called
Novecento. Since that
moment, the attitudes
became more radical, the
movement was identified
with nationalist and fascist
ideologies prevailing by
that time in Italy.

AVANT-GARDE MOVEMENTS AND GROUPS SELECTION

Denomination	Beginning	Main representatives
Impressionism	1870	Monet, Degas, Renoir, Manet, Pisarro, Sisley
Symbolism	1880	Puvis de Chavannes, Moreau; Redon
Neoimpressionism	1884	Seurat, Signac
Postimpressionism	1886	Cézanne, Gauguin, Van Gogh, Toulouse-Lautrec
Modernism	1890	Horta, Guimard, Gallé, Mackintosh, Van de Velde, Hankar, Wagner, Olbrich, Gaudi
Fauvism	1905	Matisse, Derain, Vlaminck, Dufy Braque, Roualt
Expressionism	1905	Nolde, Kirchner, Schmidt, Rottluff, Javlensky, Grosz, Dix
Cubism	1907	Picasso, Braque, Gris, Duchamp-Villon, Archipenko, Lipchitz, Zadkine
Futurism	1909	Boccioni, Balla, Carrà, Severini, Sant' Elia
Purism	1910	Le Corbusier, Ozenfant
Orphism	1912	Delaunay, (Robert y Sonia), Kupka
Gold Section	1912	Villon, Duchamp
Tubularism or Mechanicism	1912	Léger
Suprematism	1913	Malévich
Constructivism	1913	Tatlin, El Lissitzky, Pevsner, Gabo
Dadaism	1916	Janco, Arp, Duchamp, Picabia, Ernst, Schwitters, Hausmann
Metaphysical painting	1917	Chirico, Carrà, Morandi, Campigli
Neoplasticism	1917	Mondrian, Van Doesburg, Rietveld, Vantongerloo
Bauhaus	1919	Gropius, Klee, Kandinsky, Moholy-Nagy, Albers
Surrealism	1924	Dali, Magritte, Delvaux, Ernst, Tanguy, Masson, Miró, Giacometti
Abstract expressionism	1946	Pollock, Kline, De Kooning, Motherwell
Informalism	1950	Mathieu, Fautrier, Michaux, Dubuffet

Avant-Garde. Term applied to the different innovatory trends that appeared in the XXth century, both in the field of art and in the literature one.

Bodegón. (Still life). Painting genre in which there are depicted inanimated beings (dead animals, flowers, fruits or objects). The term originates in the XVIIIth century, although the genre is older.

Bronze. Tin and copper alloy. Artistic work carried out in bronze.

Canvas. Material used to paint, mainly made of linen, cotton or hempen cloth. Painting performed on canvas.

Chromatic shade. A colour intensity or luminosity rate, either by itself, or in relation with the others included in the surface of the artistic work. There exist several kind of shades: warm, cold or neutral.

Collage. French word meaning «glued». Plastic technique consisting in glueing over a support (canvas, cardboard, etc.) any kind of material, preferably paper. It was initially utilized by Picasso and Braque on their cubist works.

Colour. Impression that the sunbeams reflected by a body cause in the sensorial organs through the eye's retina. The three primary colours — blue, red and yellow — are the basis of all others, which are obtained by means of mixtures. They are considered pure when they are not mixed, lessened by the addition of black.

Composition. Organization, structure of the various elements, motifs, shapes and colours forming the artistic work.

Constructive. See **Contructivism.**

Drawing. Technique of graphic performance in which the image is traced by means of instruments such as pencils, pens, canes,etc. In most cases it is of a single colour.

Execution. Performance, elaboration of a work of art.

Figure. Artistic performance of the human or animal effigy.

Forge. Mode of working metal, mainly iron, exposing it to the fire of the forge and making it malleable with a hammer over the anvil. By extension, it is applied to forged iron work.

Form. Shape, outward appearance that involves a material. That what is seen of it through the senses or by means of a superficial inspection.

Format. Size and form of a picture, drawing, etc. Generally, there are divided in vertical and horizontal formats, and in small, medium or large formats.

Gesturalism. Generic concept to name the corporal expression gesture through which the artist carries out the painting act. It was specially esteemed by the *Action Painting* followers.

Graphism. Each artist's own way of making his strokes.

Grisaille. From the French word *grisaille*. Painting exclusively performed with the grey, white and black range. It was profusely used in the xvith century.

Iconography. Identification and description of certain artistics objects that show between them a specific coherence, either of intelectual or social kind. Likewise, iconography includes the study of the changes experienced by the said subjects all through the time and in contact with the diverse cultural fields.

Indian Ink. Fluid originally obtained from lampblack, gelatine and certain odoriferous, such as camphor or musk. It is used for drawing, providing a very solid and uniform colour. Currently the original manufacturing procedure has been replaced by others of an industrial kind.

Material. In the art critic usual language, material is understood to mean the dyestuff material, the pigment. In relation to the newest tendencies, there is a wider meaning, including any product used in the elaboration of artistic work: paper, fabric, wood, plastic and, in general, any kind of fragment and scrap.

Mixed Media. A mixture or addition of several techniques in just one artistic work.

Model. (Scale). Reproduction or sketch to scale of a sculpture or architecture.

Model. Figure or object that the artist reproduces on his work. Likewise, this term is used to designate the person who poses for painters or sculptors.

Mobile. Work of art incorporating the movement, whether produced by means of outside elements, such as the air or the spectator manipulation, or due to any kind of mechanical operation.

Motif. Subject or topic of work of art.

Movement. Wider term than «style», and which is applied to the group of artistic or ideological manifestations with certain characteristics that lend to unity, meaning a perceptible change in relation to other prior manifestations.

Oil. Painting technique used since the xvth century, consisting in dissolving the colours in an oily agglutinative, such as linseed oil, walnut or animal oils, adding hereto some volatile elements like turpentine to get a better drying. Picture painted by means of the oil technique.

Outline. Line that delimits and goes around a figure, object or composition.

Painting. Artistic tecnique that consists in the use of pigments or colours, dissolved in different elements, on a surface, with a representative, expressive or ornamental purpose. Pictorial work. That what is performed in a painting work.

Palette. Tool shovel shaped, widened out in one of its ends, generally made in wood or metal, it is utilized to paste the colours and spread them over the picture.

Paranoic-critic method. From the French term *Mèthode paranoïaque-critique*. Exploration system created by Salvador Dali during his stage of militancy in the surrealist movement, meaning a real revolution in relation with the theoretical fundament of said movement.

Perspective. Skill or technique with which it is possible to depict, in a conventional way, objects in three dimensions over a surface.

Pictorial. Art painting characteristic.

Pigment. Any kind of substance that, melted with a liquid, is transformed into a coloured matter able to be used for painting. Pigments may be organics (of animal or vegetal origin) and inorganic (minerals), although today both are artificially made.

Plane. On the picture every imaginary surface set by the objects that are depicted as placed at the same distance from the real surface of the said picture.

Plaster. Calcined gypsum that, water-mixed, is used as plastic material in the sculpture, mainly to get moulds.

Plasticity. Group of qualities of a work which makes it expressive, specially with regard to the achievement of volumetric sense.

Plein air. French expression meaning «open air». It is used to refer to the pictures performed outside the studio, to avoid artificial light. The open air painting habit was set-up as a regular practice during the Impressionism period.

Reflective disorientation. From the French term

Dépaysement réflechi.. Surrealist technique that consist in fixing the images arising from the subconcious, by forming in perfectly logical spaces — obtained through renacentist perspectives — of extraneous objects.

Relief. Sculptural work non-exempt. There are three kinds: bas, medium and high-relief.

Representation. Reproduction of the image or appearance of something.

Scene. Term utilized in the language of art critic to describe a group of figures depicted in sculptures or pictures. It is used in contrast to the depiction of separated or unrelated figures.

Scenography. Group of elements (architectural, ornamental, landscapes, etc.) that lay out in a work of art in such a way that helps to get the feeling of a particular atmosphere.

Sculpture. Art where solid materials are used to bestow a three-dimensional shape, representing in volume an object, figure or motif, real or imaginary. The work of a sculptor.

Sign. In the language of art critic, graphic which

contains by itself a semantic meaning, setting the union nexus between the conceptual and the artistic expression world.

Soldering. Solid union of one thing with another, by smelting their own material in the union point, by a smelted product of same or similar kind. Autogenous welding is the one realized without interposing any other material, smelting the edges of the two sections to be soldered.

Still life. See **Bodegón.**

Stroke. Line, stripe or dash made by pencil or brush. Delineation.

Structure. Way of placing the elements relating one with the others to form a coherent and organic whole. Group of elements that shape a structure.

Structuring. See **Structure.**

Style. Group of an artist's distinctive and persistent features, period, school or geographical area, which allow to identify the individual or collective creation.

Subject. Topic or motif about which it is the case of the work of art.

Support. Surface over which the painting work is performed. Traditionally there were mainly utilized as supports, canvas, panels or walls, but nowadays any kind of material is used.

Technique. A group of procedures and means utilized by the author to carry out his work.

Tendency.
See **Trend.**

Treatment. Method used in the elaboration of the work of art.

Trend. Group of artistic ideas or patterns directed to the same course and going after an equal purpose. They are usually stated or published by means of manifestos or programmatical writings.

Texture. Structure of an artistic work material. It might provide rugose, rough, smooth, glossy, velvety, etc. finishings.

Vanitas. Latin term meaning «vanity». Still life mode in which appear skulls, water-clocks and other elements alluding to the ephemeral human nature. Likewise, in this composition there were included inscriptions tending to emphasize the time fleetingness, as

Vanitas vanitatum, which originates this kind of denomination of pictures. The Spaniards Valdés Leal and Pereda, in the XVIIIth century, figure among its most distinguished promoters.

Version. Each one of the performances of a subject or artistic topic, as well as a musical interpretation.

Void. Cavity or hollow in a three-dimensional work of art.

Volume. Bulk, amount of space filled by something.

© ALDEASA ® 1994

Depósito legal: M-10859

ISBN: 84-8003-035-6

Design and Layout: Mar Lissón / Natàlia Arranz

General Coordinator: Ángeles Martín / Paula Casado

Translation: Alicia Lewin Amatriain

Photographs: Photographic Archives of the MNCARS. Joaquín Cortés / José Luis Municio

For authorized reproductions: © VEGAP, Madrid 1994, © DEMART PROARTE B.V.,
© FUNDACIÒ ANTONI TÀPIES, © FUNDACIÒ PILAR Y JOAN MIRÒ, © of the artists. Madrid 1994

Photocomposition: Grafitex S.A. Barcelona

Photomechanical: Lucam. Madrid

Printed in Spain by: TF. Madrid

Printed in Spain.